BEYOND THE MOONGATE

True Stories of 1920s China

Elizabeth Quan

Tundra Books

Published in Canada by Tundra Books, a division of Random House of Canada Limited,
One Toronto Street, Suite 300, Toronto, Ontario M5C 2V6

Published in the United States by Tundra Books of Northern New York,
P.O. Box 1030, Plattsburgh, New York 12901

Library of Congress Control Number: 2012934216

LIBRARY AND ARCHIVES CANADA CATALOGUING IN PUBLICATION

Quan, Elizabeth, 1921-
    Beyond the moongate / written and illustrated by Elizabeth Quan.

ISBN 978-1-77049-383-4. – ISBN 978-1-77049-382-7 (EPUB)

    1. Quan, Elizabeth, 1921- –Travel – China – Juvenile literature. 2. China – Description
and travel – Juvenile literature. 3. China – Social life and customs – 1912-1949 – Juvenile
literature. I. Title.

DS710.Q825 2013   j915.104'41   C2012-901554-7

We acknowledge the financial support of the Government of Canada through the Canada
Book Fund and that of the Government of Ontario through the Ontario Media Development
Corporation's Ontario Book Initiative. We further acknowledge the support of the Canada
Council for the Arts and the Ontario Arts Council for our publishing program.

ONTARIO ARTS COUNCIL
CONSEIL DES ARTS DE L'ONTARIO

Edited by Sue Tate
Designed by Erin Cooper
Medium: watercolor on paper

www.tundrabooks.com

Printed and bound in China

1 2 3 4 5 6   18 17 16 15 14 13

To the Lee King family and their descendants

MOONGATES DOTTED THE LANDSCAPE OF OLD CHINA.
Ancient Chinese architects designed round doorways of sculpted stone,
with the spiritual symbolism of the full moon. Stepping through one
of these doorways was to enter a world of peace and happiness. . . .

And so it was in the 1920s that the Lee King family – father,
mother, and six children, aged ten months to seven years – traveled
from their home in Canada, across the Pacific Ocean, to inland
China. There, they stepped beyond the moongate into a land not yet
touched by technology.

The story of the journey, which lasted one full cycle of the moon,
was told in *Once Upon a Full Moon*. This story, *Beyond the Moongate*,
tells of the two "golden" years the family spent with Grandmother in
a remote village in the south, which hadn't changed for centuries.

Step inside and live the long lazy days of a China forever gone.
The moongate beckons. . . .

Contents

CHINA MORNING

I sat bolt upright in bed. *Where am I?* From another part of the house, Papa's ringing voice brought it all back.

Yesterday, after a long, long trip from Canada, we arrived at Grandmother's house! Papa kowtowed to his mother to show his deep respect, and her face lit up with joy.

The house was built to accommodate two families, with a shared dining area and an open courtyard. Grandmother used one of the kitchens as her room because she liked to be at the front of the house. For her bed, she placed a board across the brick stove. Dai So, her widowed granddaughter-in-law, had a room at the back, on the other side of the house. Tall, gaunt, and unsmiling, she was a good companion for Grandmother.

Last night, when my older sister, Gerry, and I were led to Dai So's bedroom, the oil lamps made weird dancing shadows in the dark. "You will sleep here," she told us. There was a cot with a tied-back mosquito net that looked quite cozy. I kicked off my shoes and fell into bed.

This morning, Gerry was the first to get up. She showed me the covered earthen pot behind the bedroom door and the wooden basin on a stand in the courtyard. I dipped my fingers into the cold water, then went to the other side of the house to see my family.

And so, my two years in China had begun....

PIGLET COMES HOME

Popo, as we called Grandmother, rounded up her "little puppies," as she called us, to greet her new piglet. There it was – out of its cage, beside the adobe house next door. Piglet was wriggling its little pink snout, sniffing its new surroundings.

Every evening after supper, Popo would go among the villagers and collect their table scraps. Then she would boil them up for Piglet's meal of the day. How Piglet thrived!

The adobe house, built of sun-dried earth and straw, was the house where Popo had come as a bride and where Papa grew up. The front room contained a simple stone mill and a foot-operated, wooden mortar and pestle for husking and refining rice. My brothers loved to "work" these primitive machines, creating a great deal of noise and dust. The back room was Piglet's.

Lily, George, and Peter – aged four, three, and two – became Popo's new helpers. They would take Piglet out to exercise while Popo cleaned its pen. They all ran about, laughing and squealing with Piglet. Looking on, Popo laughed the loudest.

Clothes Matter

One morning, a group of girls greeted my sisters and me, eager to get a good look at the "foreign devil" children. They stared at us with great curiosity. When we'd first arrived, their grandmothers and mothers had lifted our skirts to see what we wore underneath, but the girls were too shy. They all dressed alike, in loose blouses and pants, their hair neatly braided. One of the older ones had a baby strapped on her back. The girls looked friendly, and I longed to be part of their group.

I knew this would not happen if we continued to wear clothes from Canada. So we begged for new clothes, and Mama and Dai So began a sewing marathon! Soon Gerry, Lily, and I had two new sets of blouse and pants each, stitched entirely by hand.

Later at school, I spilled black ink all down the front of one of my new white blouses. I was promptly sent home. After all her hard work, Dai So was so angry that she punished me by making me squat in the courtyard, scrubbing hopelessly for hours. "Wait until your father comes home!" she said.

New Year's Day

New Year's Day arrived, the most celebrated festival of the Chinese calendar. On this day, all debts had to be paid, no bad words could be spoken, no chopsticks could be dropped. Everyone was clean and wore new clothes. Even the house was spotless!

Just like in Canada, New Year's was a time for special food. Mama steamed a whole chicken inside a winter melon and made sweet red and green bean paste, which she stuffed into wraps as dumplings. She pressed little round dough patties onto a clean comb for texture and fried them, finally dusting them with sugar. She showed us how to wrap chopped dried oysters in fresh lettuce leaves for dipping into plum sauce. *Yum!* Then came candied melon slices – and noodles, of course, the longer the better, to signify long life.

When the noodles were ready, we were supposed to put some into our mouth with chopsticks, bite off a portion, and let the rest slide back into the soup. But I liked to suck each long noodle noisily, until the end flipped up and tickled my nose with a splash of soup!

After we ate, we went outside to hear storytellers share tales of long-ago China, of kings and feudal princes, their wars and victories and beautiful women. Some told of fairy folk in the Heavenly Realms of the Immortals. Others came for several days in a row, standing in the same spot to continue their tales. Mostly illiterate, the villagers, young and old alike, loved these stories as a way of learning about China's past.

THE CHING MING FESTIVAL

Ching Ming dawned bright and clear, marking the arrival of spring. It was a perfect day for visiting the graves of the ancestors. Dai So packed two hampers of lotus buns and bean cakes for the journey. As the men and boys milled about, I begged to go along. Women and girls were not usually granted this privilege, but Popo took my side. "What's the harm? Let her go!" she said. Papa relented, and we set off.

The way was long, rocky, and difficult. Once we passed beautiful trees in full bloom, Papa pointed out the footprint of an Immortal – a stone depression filled with water, which had shown many generations of grave visitors that they were halfway there.

At each site we visited, the men and boys raked and tidied up. We always left food for the spirits before moving on. When lunchtime came, we rested in the shade and talked about our common ancestors, forever remembered. According to Chinese beliefs, our ancestors were always there to guide and shape the destinies of their families on Earth. And so we honored them.

Chinese School

Above all, Papa wanted his children to learn to read and write Chinese, the language we spoke at home. But there was no school in the village. With permission from the Elders, Papa decided to establish one. The site he chose was a Buddhist temple, just outside the village, and he hired two teachers from the city. When he made a trip there to buy supplies, he took me with him.

On opening day, twenty-five boys and girls of all ages from a number of nearby villages attended. Gerry soon became popular by translating everybody's name into English.

I felt out of place. Although I could read *The Little Red Hen* in English, the Chinese version gave me so much trouble! On oral composition day, I was scared to death, so I skipped school and wandered about the next village until it was time for lunch. No one missed me.

At the end of the first term, I ranked almost last! The results were posted on the village bulletin board for all to see. Papa could not have been proud of me. I so hoped that Buddha and Kwan Yin, Goddess of Mercy, would look down on me from their alcove with understanding and sympathy!

PIGSTY ADVENTURE

Gerry made friends easily. I didn't, so I was always happy to follow along wherever she went. One day, we walked to the next village to visit a classmate. She lived in a humble home with an earthen floor, swept as clean and shiny as a clay pot. A fat gray hen strutted majestically about, as if she owned the place.

Our classmate's mother offered us a treat – a sweetened ground-rice mixture – to spoon onto our tongues. As it melted, our mouths filled with a burst of flavor.

Afterwards, Gerry announced, "Come on! I know a short way home." Through a maze of back lanes and alleys, we came to a low wall made of mud bricks. Scaling it easily, we dropped straight into our neighbor's pigsty! The mother pig, a fat sow, grunted, but neither she nor her piglet minded us being there.

All of a sudden, the owner came running and shouting at the top of her voice: "What are you two doing to my pigs? You're frightening them! I'm going to tell your grandmother!"

Here Comes the Bride

The news spread like wildfire. A bridal sedan was entering the village gates! Just before, two men had carried in the trousseau — the collection of gifts the bride was bringing to her new home. Now the bridal sedan lurched along the narrow lane as it was carried up the village walk. Its red tassels bobbed and swayed, and the curtains trembled.

The beautiful red sedan, decorated in gold, concealed the "jewel" within — some lovely maiden being borne to the home of her soon-to-be husband, whom she had never met face-to-face.

We happily joined the throng of children following behind, hoping to catch sight of the bride. As she alighted to cries of "The bride, the bride!" we glimpsed a dainty figure in red silk, crowned with a jeweled headdress. She was hurriedly escorted through a decorated doorway as the sound of firecrackers filled the air.

Makeup Time

Gerry and I were curious. *Was the bride one of the pretty older girls in our school from another village? And was the groom one of the nice young men who helped me jump over the crevasse on the Ching Ming walk? Hmm. . . .* We decided to find out by paying the bride a visit.

The next day, we proceeded to the house with the decorated doorway. Although we did not know her, the bride was glad to see us and invited us in. With no duties to perform for her mother-in-law yet, she dawdled with her makeup and her jar of fine-toothed combs at her dressing table. "Shall I make you pretty?" she asked.

Gerry and I smiled and nudged each other, unsure of what she had in mind. But soon she began to apply powder, rouge, and lipstick, chatting all the while. She told us she was seventeen and how much she was enjoying transforming us. Then she dabbed flower-scented dew behind our ears so we would smell pretty, too. When she had finished, we carefully examined ourselves in the mirror – *gorgeous!* We hurried home to show Mama.

She took one horrified look. *"Ai yah!!"* she screamed, running for a washcloth and soap.

MOSES

Dai So's adopted son, Moses, had been away at school, but came home during the school break. A handsome boy of fifteen, he provided us with so much amusement.

First, he taught us how to catch fireflies and put them into a jar, their beautiful green incandescence glowing in the dark. Then he showed us how to find crickets, especially ones that might become fighters. We searched for males with powerful heads, long legs, and loud, ringing chirps. Moses had a champion in a bamboo cage, which he kept for challenging his friends' fighter crickets. He took it out to show us, letting it crawl from one hand to the other and teasing it with a blade of grass. It was ferocious-looking, opening and closing its fangs and waving its whiskers. It had won many battles.

Moses taught us how to make reed whistles. What a sight we must have been, trailing behind him and blowing our noisemakers! He opened up a whole new world for us.

We especially liked to watch him shower. He would fill pails with water from the well, roll up his pants, then lather up, singing at the top of his lungs. He would pour the water over his head, one pail at a time, letting it flow down the open sewer in front of the house to the pond. We all laughed with glee. Showering was a totally new concept for us – we did not shower, even in Canada. Here we washed from a wooden bucket. Running water would not come to the village for another fifty years.

PIRATE ALERT

Popo's village was near the southern coast of Kwangtung province. Pirates roamed the South China Sea, sometimes coming up onto the rich Pearl River delta to plunder the bounty of the villages.

One day, when Papa was chatting with the Elders at the ancestral temple as usual, a runner arrived with news of a pirate landing. Papa rushed home. "Hurry, everyone, into the hiding place at once!" he shouted, brandishing his gun.

When Papa renovated the house, he'd installed a partition to conceal a secret space accessible from the second floor through a trapdoor. Ventilation was provided through a tiny window high up on the wall, visible only from the back lane.

Dai So opened the trapdoor and herded us all down the steep, narrow stairs to the dark, dank space below. We went down backwards, feeling our way, Mama carrying the youngest. Last one in, Dai So closed the trapdoor.

We stood there in the dark side by side, pressed silently against the wall, hearts pounding. We waited, trembling, afraid.

Finally, we heard Papa's voice: "Come out now! All is clear!"

New Baby Brother

When my new baby brother was born, I was sound asleep. In the morning, Papa came to tell us, "You have a new brother. He was born in the Hour of the Rat. He will be very independent!"

We hurried over to the other side of the house and saw this tiny infant all wrapped up in old clothes, in accordance with Chinese tradition, to deceive evil spirits. The baby's eyes were tightly closed. Mama was smiling. Now we were seven — four girls and three boys. Papa was so proud of his third son.

Gerry loved the new baby right away and begged to carry it around, strapped to her back. Dai So produced an embroidered baby carrier, with bands to tie around the body. She helped with the knots, and, before long, Gerry was carrying the baby wherever she went.

At the baby's One Month Banquet, Papa invited the whole village for a celebratory feast, which also served as a housewarming for the renovated house. People came throughout the day, including beggars from near and far.

There was a whole pig, roasted on a spit, baskets of fish balls to be mixed with cooked greens, and a great cauldron of rice. My brothers, George and Peter, loved the fish balls and helped themselves again and again. No one scolded them, for in the land beyond the moongate, children were allowed to be children.

Chinese Herbalist

My reaction to the birth of my new baby brother was entirely different from Gerry's. I wanted more of Mama's and Papa's attention, so I pretended to have a bad stomachache. They made me special soup and piggybacked me to bed. When Papa took me to see a Western doctor in Dai Jok, a nearby town, the doctor tapped all over my bare tummy.

"Does it hurt here?"

"Yes."

"Does it hurt here?

"No."

"Here?"

"Yes."… "No."… "Yes." *Tap-tap.*

When the Western doctor could not diagnose my "illness," my parents sent to the mountains for a famous herbalist. I was stretched out and held down on a day sofa, with my tummy exposed. The herbalist decided to treat me with "moxibustion." He prepared a mix of powdered herbs, placed it on a slice of ginger on my belly button, and – horror of horrors – he lit it! Smoke curled up in a sizzling spiral. Terrified, I leapt up, instantly cured!

How wise the herbalist was in his craft. He knew what I wanted: *Notice me, Mama. It's number-two daughter – I exist, too!*

MOONGATE HOUSE

My favorite spot to play was in the walled garden of a two-storey redbrick house at the edge of the village. We called it Moongate House because of the large moon-shaped window on the veranda that faced the fishpond. During the renovation of Popo's house, we all lived there. The house belonged to my uncle, who was then in Canada. Popo grew vegetables here, and while we played, she kept an eye on the little ones to make sure they didn't go too near the water.

The fishpond was magical to us. It teemed with goldfish, darting in and out of the shadows cast by the bamboo grove beside it. Mama had taught us how to fold paper to make little boats, and we sailed armadas of them in the water.

Often we noticed snakes moving among the bamboo stalks, but they did not harm us. A large longan tree stood proudly by the gate, providing a perfect place to climb. What a paradise! When the tree became laden with sweet fruit, Popo would place a board under it to sleep on and guard the harvest.

CANTONESE OPERA

Women were not allowed onstage. Yet Papa was captivated by the "beauties" who performed there. They would sway back and forth, their feet strapped into wooden contraptions, so that when they walked, they looked like women with bound feet. The impersonators were beautifully made up and dressed in vibrant costumes. Accompanied by wailing string instruments, they sang their hearts out, using falsetto to imitate female voices.

The performing troupes toured everywhere. One came to Dai Jok, which was close to Popo's village. Papa loved this form of entertainment, so he went every day, sometimes coming home very late. Mama worried, for the fear of bandits was real indeed. She kept watch at an upstairs window, and Lily often watched with her.

One day, Mama took Gerry and me out of school so we could take a train to Dai Jok to attend a performance. We got all dressed up, but as we passed the school and heard the other children reciting their lessons, we felt guilty. *Oh well,* we thought, *we don't do this every day!*

In town, the sight of the stalls and the milling of the crowds thrilled us – so different from an ordinary day in our village!

Popo the Healer

Popo, our beloved grandmother, was an extraordinary woman, well-known to a wide community of villages on the Pearl River delta. A staunch Christian, she'd had contact with missionaries from an early age. Her home had become the headquarters for Christian villagers from far and wide to gather for fellowship, service, and prayer.

Prayer was Popo's lifeblood, and she used it to heal others. People in sickness or distress would send for her from great distances, and she would set out on foot with a companion. One devoted woman told me that, once, when she and Popo arrived too late, Popo prayed through the long night. By morning, the "dead" man was brought back to life!

Though Popo had little money, she was known to give her train fare away so someone less fortunate could ride to the church located in town, several miles away. Popo would walk there on her own bound feet. In later years, she'd saved enough to build a small church at the edge of her village.

Popo's eyes were keen and her ears alert. She could hear a raucous disturbance from a great distance and would run outside, banging her iron pot with a bamboo stick, to alert everyone to trouble. Once, when bandits came to the village, pounding up the main walkway and thundering by with their swords and long knives gleaming in the moonlight, they avoided her house. It was told that an angel was perched on her rooftop.

Good-bye, Popo

Papa's two-year visa was running out. We knew there was not much time left with Grandmother. But we had a big problem: the new baby, born in China, could not legally be brought back to Canada. *How could we leave him behind? Who would look after him?*

Time was precious now, and we felt a sense of foreboding. There seemed to be no solution to our problem. Papa devised a plan – my youngest sister, Etta, would stay in China with the baby.

The day came to leave. Mama had put out our clothes from Canada the night before, and we dressed as soon as we arose. Papa had sent our luggage on ahead.

When I looked at Papa, he had a funny, pinched look on his face. Etta and the baby had been taken to a neighbor's to spare Mama the grief of saying good-bye. As we hurried toward the village gates, Mama was close to tears. I turned to look back.

Popo was standing alone at the end of the lane, waving bravely, tears streaming down her wrinkled brown face.

Don't cry, Popo, I thought. *Etta and the baby are waiting for you. They need your love and comfort. They will make you smile. Dear, sweet Popo, I will always love you. Good-bye, good-bye forever!*

And so our time in China had come to an end.

Afterword

Grandmother lived, in good health, to be almost one hundred years old. One day, to escape marauding Japanese, she climbed a tree, fell,

and died of complications from the injury. It took another seven years for our family to be reunited. Through the kindness of our local MP, Hugh Cleaver, a special dispensation from Ottawa permitted our "baby" brother to be brought to Canada. A few years later, an uncle accompanied him, then eight, along with our sister Etta.

Papa took us to China to introduce us to the land of his birth and the ties that bound him there. Even though I was born in Canada ninety years ago and spent most of my life here, deep in my heart I have a warm feeling for the land of our ancestors; for the magical land beyond the moongate; and for its people, the Hans, forever rooted to that land.